W9-BEY-521

21st
Century
Skills Library

ROAD TO RECOVERY

BALD EAGLE

Susan H. Gray

Cherry Lake Publishing
Ann Arbor, Michigan

Published in the United States of America by Cherry Lake Publishing
Ann Arbor, Michigan
www.cherrylakepublishing.com

Content Adviser: Robert Hatcher, Chairman, National Bald Eagle Grant
Advisory Team, American Eagle Foundation

Photo Credits: Cover and page 1, ©FloridaStock, used under license from Shutterstock,
Inc.; page 4, ©Peter Arnold, Inc./Alamy; pages 6 and 25, ©Juniors Bildarchiv/Alamy;
page 8, ©Tony Campbell, used under license from Shutterstock, Inc.; page 9, ©Danita
Delimont/Alamy; page 10, ©Martin Smart/Alamy; page 13, ©The Natural History
Museum/Alamy; page 14, ©nialat, used under license from Shutterstock, Inc.; page 16,
©Charles Melton/Alamy; page 19, ©Cornforth Images/Alamy; page 20, ©HTuller, used
under license from Shutterstock, Inc.; page 22, ©Victor Fraile/Alamy; page 26, ©David
Gowans/Alamy

Map by XNR Productions Inc.

Library of Congress Cataloging-in-Publication Data

Gray, Susan Heinrichs.
Bald eagle / Susan H. Gray.
   p. cm.—(Road to recovery)
Includes index.
ISBN-13: 978-1-60279-317-0
ISBN-10: 1-60279-317-4
1. Bald eagle—Juvenile literature. I. Title.
QL696.F32G73 2009
598.9'42—dc22   2008028613

Cherry Lake Publishing would like to acknowledge the work of
The Partnership for 21st Century Skills.
Please visit www.21stcenturyskills.org *for more information.*

TABLE OF CONTENTS

CHAPTER ONE

THE BIG DAY

Young bald eagles do not look like adult bald eagles.

This is the big day. The young bald eagle (*Haliaeetus leucocephalus*) is taking her first long flight. She has spent the first 3 months of her life in this nest, and now she is ready to leave. Over the last few weeks, she has first stretched and then flapped her wings. In recent days, she has flown in place over her nest. Her wing and chest muscles have grown stronger. Her flapping motions have become smooth and controlled.

The breezes on this warm day are perfect. She spreads her wings, faces into the wind, and lifts into the sky.

Charles Broley was a Canadian banker and a bird lover. He often escaped the cold weather by spending the winter months in Florida. While in Florida, he spent long days bird-watching. Bald eagles were among his favorites. He loved how majestic and powerful they looked. He enjoyed watching them soar high in the sky. But in the late 1940s, after about a decade of studying bald eagles, he noticed something was wrong. Of the many eagle pairs he watched, only a few had young. The Florida population was slowly dwindling. Broley's observation led scientists to discover that harmful **pesticides** were in the environment. The pesticides were causing the birds to disappear.

CHAPTER TWO

LIFE OF THE BALD EAGLE

Bald eagles have very sharp vision. They can spot prey, such as fish, from high in the air.

The bald eagle is a large bird that is found throughout much of North America. Populations exist in Canada, Alaska, the lower 48 states, and northern Mexico. The birds live near bodies of water where they can find their main food—fish. Bald eagles also **prey** on small animals such as rabbits, squirrels, and ducks.

Adults usually weigh between 6.5 and 14 pounds (2.9 and 6.4 kilograms). They have a wingspan of about 6 to 8 feet (1.8 to 2.4 meters). Females are usually larger than males. Except for the white head and tail, the body is covered with brown feathers. The adult eagle's beak is yellow and hooks downward at the tip. The legs and feet are also yellow, and each toe ends in a sharp, curved **talon**.

Eagles hunt by perching high in a treetop or on a bluff. They scan the area with their sharp eyes. When they spot the glint of sunlight on a fish or the movement of a rabbit, they swoop down quickly. They snag the prey with their sharp talons and carry it away, often taking it to a nest to feed their young.

A bald eagle starts life in a very large nest, known as an **aerie**. Eagle pairs usually build their nests near the tops of

Bald eagles build large nests.

tall trees. Rarely, an eagle pair will nest on a rocky cliff or

on the ground. A new aerie is about 5 feet (1.5 m) across

and about 2 feet (0.6 m) deep. Once they build a nest, the

pair may return to it year after year, adding sticks, twigs,

Eagles choose cliffs as nesting sites in areas without tall trees.

moss, and feathers. The nest grows larger every year. Some

nests end up weighing more than a ton!

Females lay up to three dull white eggs in the nest. The

adults take turns sitting on the eggs. After about 5 weeks, the

eggs begin to hatch. **Hatchlings** are weak birds, covered with

An adult eagle feeds two eaglets. Baby eagles grow quickly
and gain about 1 pound (0.5 kg) per week.

light gray fluffy feathers, or down. The parents share duties.

While one parent cares for the hatchlings, the other adult

hunts for food for itself and the young. When the adults are in the nest, they carefully step around their young. This keeps their sharp talons from piercing the chicks.

Eaglets grow rapidly. By the time they are 12 weeks old, they are as large as their parents. At about 10 to 12 weeks of age, the young eagles begin hopping around the nest and flapping their wings with their faces to the wind. By this time, they have lost their down and are covered with dark brown feathers.

An eaglet's first flight is usually short. It may almost lose its balance on its first landing. Soon, however, the eaglet becomes more graceful and begins taking longer flights. It also tests its hunting skills, killing small prey such as frogs. About 1 month after its first flight, an eaglet leaves home for good.

When an eagle is about 4 to 5 years old, white feathers replace the brown ones on its head and tail. The eagle is now an adult and begins looking for a mate. Bald eagles

mate for life. But if one of the pair dies, the other finds a new mate. In the wild, about half of bald eagles die during their first year. This is mainly because they are too young to know how to survive dangerous situations. If they survive their first year, bald eagles have been known to live as long as 39 years in the wild.

CHAPTER THREE

THE EAGLES BEGIN TO VANISH

Artist John James Audubon created this portrait of a bald eagle in the 19th century.

Between 1804 and 1806, explorers Meriwether Lewis and William Clark traveled the wilds of the American West. They noted that there were a lot of bald eagles in some

The eagle became the national symbol of the United States in 1782.

places and wrote that the birds had "many nests in the tall cottonwood trees." Scientists today believe that more than 100,000 bald eagles lived in the lower 48 United States at that time. But over the next 150 years, eagle numbers dropped dangerously low. By 1960, the national bird was in danger of becoming **extinct**. How did this happen?

The trouble began as more people settled throughout the country. Between 1800 and 1900, the U.S. population increased by about 70 million people. They cleared land, created farms and ranches, and built towns and cities. With or without realizing it, many people did things that caused the bald eagle population to shrink.

Some of the settlers shot the birds. They thought that bald eagles were a threat to their livestock. Sometimes, the eagles ate other animals that had been shot with **ammunition** containing lead. When they did this, they took the lead into their own bodies. Over time, they became poisoned by the lead and died.

In the 20th century, things got much worse. That's when many people began using pesticides to kill harmful insects. In particular, people used a chemical with a long name

DDT entered the bodies of bald eagles when they ate fish contaminated with the pesticide.

that was called DDT for short. It killed many insects that destroyed plants or carried disease. DDT turned out to be one of the biggest causes of the decline in bald eagle numbers.

DDT was not sprayed on eagles, so how did it cause so much harm? It came to the eagles through water and the **food chain.** Each time farmers sprayed DDT on their crops, the chemical landed on the plants and on the ground. When it rained, the DDT washed into streams, rivers, and lakes. Fish took it into their bodies, and so did animals that drank the water. Bald eagles ate those fish and other animals. DDT began to build up in the bald eagles' bodies.

In female eagles, DDT had a terrible effect. The poison interfered with the formation of the shells of their eggs. The females laid eggs with weak shells that broke easily. Because so many eggs broke, the total number of bald eagle chicks shrank.

Learning & Innovation Skills

In 1948, the Swiss chemist Paul Müller received an international prize for his work on DDT. He showed that the chemical could greatly benefit human beings. DDT killed some of the insects that destroyed crops. This helped farmers to be more productive. The chemical also killed mosquitoes. These insects are not just pests; they also carry a disease called **malaria**. People with malaria have fever, chills, and headaches, and many die. In the 1940s and 1950s, the spraying of DDT probably saved millions of lives around the world. Today, many people still die from malaria. Do you think DDT should still be used to prevent malaria? Why or why not?

The eagles also faced other problems. As cities grew, some of the birds' **habitat** was destroyed. Large trees that provided nesting space were cut down. Eagles sometimes collided with new power lines that went up. Factories released chemicals, such as mercury, into the air and water. The chemicals caused many animals, including some bald eagles, to die. By 1963, eagle experts believed there were fewer than 500 bald eagle pairs in the lower 48 states.

CHAPTER FOUR

A BUMPY RECOVERY

Eagles gather at Alaska's Chilkat Bald Eagle Preserve. Protecting places where eagles live has been an important part of eagle recovery plans.

By 1940, it was clear that the bald eagles needed

protection. In that year, the U.S. government passed

the Bald Eagle Protection Act. This law made it illegal

Golden eagles have smaller heads and bills than bald eagles.

to kill, trap, disturb, buy, sell, trade, or ship any bald eagle. The law also prohibited anyone from bothering the eagles' eggs and nests. People who broke this law would have to pay a fine. They might also go to prison. The law was later changed to include golden eagles. It was renamed the Bald and Golden Eagle Protection Act.

In 1966, U.S. lawmakers passed the Endangered Species **Preservation** Act. It called for the creation of a list of endangered animals. It also said that government wildlife experts must protect the listed animals and their habitats. In 1967, the bald eagle was placed on this list.

21st Century Content

Native Americans have used eagle feathers in their religious ceremonies for years. When eagles gained protection under the law, there was no way for Native Americans to legally obtain new feathers. To solve this problem, the U.S. government created the National Eagle **Repository** in Denver, Colorado. When people discover bald and golden eagles that have died, they notify wildlife authorities. The authorities ship the birds and any loose feathers to the repository. There, workers identify the species of eagle, estimate its age, and describe its condition. They also give each bird an identification number.

Native Americans wishing to receive an eagle or eagle parts must fill out an application form. The wait is long, however. The repository receives about 1,000 eagles each year, and there are about 5,000 people on the waiting list.

Layers of feathers help keep bald eagles warm in cold weather.

The Bald Eagle Protection Act and the Endangered Species Preservation Act were good first steps toward saving the eagles. But the use of DDT made the laws almost meaningless. Beginning in the early 1940s, farmers were spraying DDT on their crops. Health officials were spraying DDT along coastlines to kill mosquitoes and stop the spread of malaria.

DDT use continued for almost 30 years. Millions of pounds of it were applied each year. By the time that people realized the chemical was harmful to wildlife, it was almost too late. The bald eagle population was already dangerously low when people made the connection between fragile eggshells and DDT.

The U.S. government banned the use of DDT in 1972. By that time, the bald eagle was already on the government's list of endangered species. Only a few hundred bald eagle pairs remained in the lower 48 states. So the government created a plan to help the species recover.

21st Century Content

After DDT was banned in the United States, the bald eagle population began to increase. By 1995, there were about 4,500 nesting pairs in the lower 48 states. The Fish and Wildlife Service said the bald eagle was no longer endangered. It was taken off the endangered species list and put on the list of threatened species.

Threatened species still need protection, and the government continued to provide it. As a result, bald eagle numbers continued to rise. In June 2007, the Fish and Wildlife Service announced that there were almost 10,000 breeding pairs in the lower 48 states. Every state had at least one pair, and some states had more than 1,000! It was time to remove bald eagles from the list.

The U.S. Fish and Wildlife Service was in charge of the plan. Service officials divided the country into five recovery regions. They set population goals for each region. They knew that the ban on DDT would help the eagles recover, but they also knew that more should be done. So service workers asked for help from state governments, Native Americans, landowners, and other groups. These groups agreed to help safeguard the bald eagles' habitat and to keep track of local eagle populations. They also decided to help educate the public about eagle protection.

CHAPTER FIVE

It's Not Over Yet!

A sign reminds people to respect the eagles and their habitat.

The Endangered Species Act of 1973 expanded the protection for endangered plants and animals. It says that the Fish and Wildlife Service must keep an eye on delisted species for 5 years. This is to make sure that those species

Some wildlife experts work with injured eagles. This bald eagle was fitted with an artificial beak after being wounded by a poacher.

remain safe and do not become endangered again. In the case of the bald eagle, the Fish and Wildlife Service is keeping track for 20 years.

Members of the Fish and Wildlife Service are not the only people protecting the bald eagle. In the late 1980s, several organizations came together to figure out how to keep large birds from colliding with power lines and poles. At the time, cranes, eagles, and other large birds often were killed when they flew into power company equipment. The group wanted to stop this from happening. Group members included people from the U.S. Fish and Wildlife Service, the National Audubon Society, and several electric companies. They became known as the **Avian** Power Line Interaction Committee, or APLIC.

APLIC members studied large birds and how they land, perch, and walk on power poles. They measured the birds' wingspans and the distances between their feet when standing. They also learned which kinds of birds build nests on the poles. Based on what they learned, they designed safer poles. On these poles, the electrical parts are covered or are difficult to reach. APLIC members share their ideas with many power companies around the country.

It's a big job to keep track of thousands of bald eagle pairs. So how does the Fish and Wildlife Service do it? They get help from state and private wildlife agencies all over the country. Wildlife experts at these agencies keep track of the pairs in their own states. They know where the old nests are and they keep an eye out for new ones. They notice when pairs are raising chicks. They report everything back to the Fish and Wildlife Service. When different groups work together like this, it helps to ensure that endangered species have a good chance of recovery.

Their designs have greatly reduced the number of eagle deaths related to electrical lines and poles. Now, companies that put up windmills are looking at APLIC's suggestions. They want to see if they can learn how to make their own structures safer.

Over the years, many people have worked to save the bald eagle. Everyone wants to make sure that our national bird is safe for decades to come.

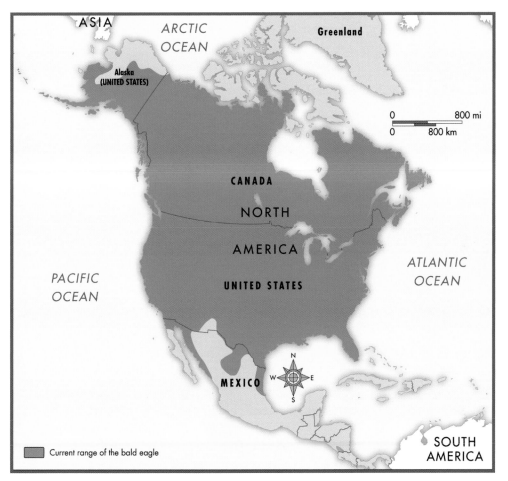

This map shows where bald eagles live in North America.

GLOSSARY

aerie (AIR-ee) the nest of a large bird of prey

ammunition (am-yuh-NISH-uhn) things, such as bullets, that are fired from weapons

avian (AY-vee-un) having to do with birds

endangered (en-DAYN-jurd) in danger of dying out completely

extinct (ex-TINGKT) the state of having died out completely

food chain (FOOD CHAYN) the series of organisms that feed on one another

habitat (HAB-uh-tat) the place where an animal or plant naturally lives and grows

hatchlings (HATCH-leengz) animals that have just hatched from an egg

malaria (muh-LAIR-ee-uh) a sometimes deadly disease transferred to humans by mosquitoes

pesticides (PESS-tuh-sydz) chemicals used to kill pests, especially insect pests

preservation (preh-zur-VAY-shun) the state of being kept safe

prey (PRAY) to hunt and eat other animals

repository (rih-POZ-ih-tor-ee) a place where things are stored

species (SPEE-sheez) a group of similar plants or animals

talon (TAL-un) the sharp claw of a bird of prey such as an eagle or hawk

For More Information

Books

Dell, Pamela. *The Bald Eagle*. Minneapolis: Compass Point Books, 2004.

Hicks, Terry Allan. *The Bald Eagle*. Tarrytown, NY: Benchmark Books, 2006.

Warhol, Tom, and Chris Reiter. *Eagles*. Tarrytown, NY: Benchmark Books, 2004.

Web Sites

American Eagle Foundation

www.eagles.org

For all kinds of information about eagles

Kids Planet—Bald Eagle

www.kidsplanet.org/factsheets/bald_eagle.html

For a description of the life and behavior of the bald eagle

National Geographic Kids—Bald Eagle Creature Feature

kids.nationalgeographic.com/Animals/CreatureFeature/Baldeagle

To learn more about bald eagles and see photographs and videos of them

U.S. Fish and Wildlife Service—Kids' Corner

www.fws.gov/Endangered/kids/index.html

For a U.S. Fish and Wildlife Service page for kids with links to "Species in the Spotlight,"
including bald eagles

INDEX

ABOUT THE AUTHOR

Susan H. Gray has a master's degree in zoology. She has written more than 90 science and reference books for children, and especially loves writing about animals. Susan also likes to garden and play the piano. She lives in Cabot, Arkansas, with her husband Michael and many pets.